FAITH HILL

A Real-Life Reader Biography

Ann Gaines

Mitchell Lane Publishers, Inc.

P.O. Box 619
Bear, Delaware 19701

Mitchell Lane
PUBLISHERS

First Printing

Real-Life Reader Biographies

Paula Abdul	Mary Joe Fernandez	Ricky Martin	Arnold Schwarzenegger
Christina Aguilera	Andres Galarraga	Mark McGwire	Selena
Marc Anthony	Sarah Michelle Gellar	Alyssa Milano	Maurice Sendak
Drew Barrymore	Jeff Gordon	Mandy Moore	Dr. Seuss
Brandy	Mia Hamm	Chuck Norris	Shakira
Garth Brooks	Melissa Joan Hart	Tommy Nuñez	Alicia Silverstone
Kobe Bryant	Jennifer Love Hewitt	Rosie O'Donnell	Jessica Simpson
Sandra Bullock	**Faith Hill**	Rafael Palmeiro	Sinbad
Mariah Carey	Hollywood Hogan	Gary Paulsen	Jimmy Smits
Cesar Chavez	Katie Holmes	Freddie Prinze, Jr.	Sammy Sosa
Christopher Paul Curtis	Enrique Iglesias	Julia Roberts	Britney Spears
Roald Dahl	Derek Jeter	Robert Rodriguez	Sheryl Swoopes
Oscar De La Hoya	Steve Jobs	J.K. Rowling	Shania Twain
Trent Dimas	Michelle Kwan	Keri Russell	Liv Tyler
Celine Dion	Bruce Lee	Winona Ryder	Robin Williams
Sheila E.	Jennifer Lopez	Cristina Saralegui	Vanessa Williams
Gloria Estefan	Cheech Marin		Tiger Woods

Library of Congress Cataloging-in-Publication Data
Gaines, Ann.
     Faith Hill/Ann Gaines.
         p. cm.—(Real-life reader biography)
     Includes discography (p.) and index.
     ISBN 1-58415-091-2
     1. Hill, Faith, 1967—Juvenile literature. 2. Country musicians—United States—Biography—Juvenile literature. [1. Hill, Faith, 1967- 2. Singers. 3. Country music.] I. Title. II. Series.
ML3930.H53 G35 2001
782.421642'092—dc21
[B]   2001029453

ABOUT THE AUTHOR: Ann Graham Gaines holds graduate degrees in American Civilization and Library and Information Science from the University of Texas at Austin. She has been a freelance writer for 18 years, specializing in nonfiction for children. She lives near Gonzales, Texas with her husband and their four children.

PHOTO CREDITS: cover: Glenn Weiner/Shooting Star; p. 4 Globe Photos; p. 6 Globe Photos; p. 18 Shooting Star; p. 24 Shooting Star; p. 25 Lisa Rose/Globe Photos; p. 28 Ron Davis/Shooting Star.

ACKNOWLEDGMENTS: The following story has been thoroughly researched, and to the best of our knowledge, represents a true story. While every possible effort has been made to ensure accuracy, the publisher will not assume liability for damages caused by inaccuracies in the data, and makes no warranty on the accuracy of the information contained herein. This story has not been authorized nor endorsed by Faith Hill.

Table of Contents

Chapter 1
One Hundred
Million People

Singer Faith Hill was still a very young child when she discovered she loved to sing and started to dream of becoming a country music star some day. Way back then, her audiences were tiny as she sang for her relatives at family reunions in her hometown of Star, Mississippi.

She sang in front of strangers for the first time when she was 7, at a mother-daughter luncheon hosted by the local 4H club. As she grew up, she got more and more experience singing in her church choir.

Faith Hill has always dreamed of being a singing star.

In 1996, Faith performed in Washington, DC for the Christmas in Washington program.

When she was a teenager, she sang with a band that performed at rodeos and county fairs. One time she even performed the "Star-Spangled Banner," our country's National Anthem, at a tobacco-spitting contest in Raleigh, Mississippi. That audience probably numbered no more than one hundred people.

Since then, her audiences have grown by a huge number. Fans purchase millions of copies of her four albums. They buy tickets to see her in concert. Radio listeners call up disc jockeys, asking them to play her songs.

The most amazing thing about this is that although Faith Hill is a country singer, fans of pop music also request her hits. She has become a crossover sensation, appealing to people who like more than one kind of music.

She has won fans all over the world. The first time the whole world got to see her on television was in 1996, when she sang at the closing ceremonies

When she was a teenager, she sang with a band that performed at rodeos and county fairs.

In 2000, Faith sang the National Anthem at the Super Bowl.

of the Summer Olympics in Atlanta, Georgia. Millions of viewers tuned in.

In 2000, the world watched again as she sang the National Anthem at the Super Bowl. She may have started singing to just a few people back in Star, Mississippi, which had a population of 2,500. But at the Super Bowl an audience of one hundred million watched her on television. That's about as big as you can get.

Chapter 2
Growing Up

Faith Hill was born on September 21, 1967, in Jackson, Mississippi. When she was still a very tiny infant, only one week old, her mother gave her up for adoption. Some women choose adoption when they find themselves pregnant at a young age or for some other reason feel unable to raise a child. When she was growing up, Faith never knew the names of her birth mother or her father, or why her mother could not raise her herself.

Her adoptive parents, Ted and Edna Perry, named their new baby Audrey Faith Perry. She joined the

Faith was adopted by Ted and Edna Perry when she was just a baby.

Perrys' two boys, Wesley and Steve. The Perrys immediately loved their little baby, who grew up using her middle rather than her first name and was known as Faith Perry.

Faith's family was very close. Her parents worked hard but spent a great deal of time with their children. Her father had a job in a factory. Faith's mother was a bank teller. Even with their two incomes, the Perry family often had little money. But Faith remembers that her mother was an expert at stretching what they had. They seldom lacked for what they needed.

The family faithfully attended church, where Faith sang in the choir from an early age. She always loved gospel music. After she became famous, one of her friends recalled that when Faith sang a hymn a cappella (all by herself, without a piano or organ to accompany her), members of the congregation would cry.

The Perrys also liked to get together with friends and their huge extended family. It was at these family reunions that Faith got her start singing. Her mother would pay her a quarter to perform. The family all loved to listen to music—Faith remembers growing up listening to Elvis Presley, Tammy Wynette, George Strait, and Reba McEntire.

At age 5, Faith started kindergarten. Because Star is too small to have its own schools, the children went to one in a nearby town. Faith made friends easily and her teachers liked her, too.

When she was in first grade, Faith joined the 4H Club, whose members raise farm animals to display at stock shows. When her club sponsored a mother-daughter luncheon, she got up and sang there. This was her first public appearance.

Faith continued to sing as she grew older, even though she had become self-conscious because she was growing very tall and skinny. Faith attended McLaurin High School, which is located in the town

Her performing career actually got started at her family reunions where her mother would pay her a quarter to sing.

of Florence, close to Star. Today it remains a small school. There are just 1,200 students in total in the McLaurin school district. A single building houses its junior high and high school classes. In high school, she was a cheerleader and president of her class. She also liked drama and sports.

And she continued to dream of one day being a singer. She joined a band, which performed locally at places like county fairs and rodeos.

Like most teenagers, Faith rebelled a little. While she was generally well behaved and stayed out of trouble, she confesses that she could act like a daredevil, too. Late at night she and her friends toilet-papered neighbors' yards, and she liked to drive fast.

Chapter 3
Getting into Country Music

After Faith graduated from high school in 1985, she enrolled in a local community college, but dropped out after just one semester. She knew deep down she really did not want to study for any other job. Her heart was set on becoming a singer. Looking back, she remembers having that dream "almost since I started talking."

Her parents, loving as always, helped her out. Her dad gave her a ride to Nashville, Tennessee, in his pick-up truck. Just eighty miles north of Mississippi's border, Nashville is

After high school, Faith enrolled at the local community college but knew it was not what she wanted.

nicknamed "Music City, USA." It's the home of the Grand Ole Opry, the best place in the world to see country music performed live. All the great country music stars have performed on its stage at one time or another.

Like so many others, Faith hoped to make it big in Music City, USA. Because she was so young and inexperienced, she thought this would be easy. "I really believed I'd just get on the Grand Ole Opry stage, start singin', and be on a bus travelin' the next day," she remembered almost ten years later.

Faith wanted to go to Nashville and sing at the Grand Ole Opry.

But there were many other people in Nashville who also wanted to be singers. Faith quickly realized that it would take longer than she had expected to get started in the music business. In the meantime, she needed a job so she could earn enough money to support herself.

It took her some time to find a job because she made a mistake in her first interviews. She would tell prospective employers about her dreams of appearing at the Grand Ole Opry. People didn't want to hire an aspiring singer. They thought she would not take her job seriously.

So she figured out that she should talk about how hard she would work. Soon she landed a job selling T-shirts. While the work was not very exciting or challenging, it provided her with the paychecks she needed.

Other jobs followed, but none of them paid very well. While she waited for the huge success she still believed would come one day, she made do, eating macaroni and cheese and hamburger.

Eventually she found a job as a receptionist in the office of Gary Morris, a country singer who had a major hit, the song *The Wind Beneath My Wings*. Besides performing for audiences, he had also written many songs (one he would write later was included in the Broadway musical, *Les Miserables*). In Nashville, he ran a music publishing business in addition to being a singer.

It took a bit longer than she had expected to get started in the music business.

Landing a job with him was a big deal for Faith because she finally had opened a door to the music business.

And getting her foot in the door would pay off. One day after Faith had been working at Morris's office for about a year, one of her fellow workers overheard her singing along with the radio. He was so impressed with her voice that he talked her into recording a demo—a demonstration tape designed to show what a singer can do. Her demo was of a song called "It Scares Me." When Gary Morris heard it, he was impressed, too. He told her she had talent and helped her find work singing in clubs and other places.

It was during this period, in 1988, that Faith made another big step in life. She married Dan Hill, who also worked for a music publishing company. Faith was just 20 years old. Later on, she would acknowledge that she was far too young for marriage.

After marrying Hill, she got another break. She met another

established singer and songwriter named Gary Burr. While he has never made a really big record, his songs have been recorded by huge country music stars like George Jones, Garth Brooks, and LeAnn Rimes. Burr sometimes asked Faith to perform with him as a backup singer. Faith landed more and more gigs, singing in bars and clubs in the Nashville area.

One night in 1992, Faith Hill was singing with Gary Burr in a famous Nashville nightspot called the Bluebird Cafe. An executive with Warner Brothers Records named Martha Sharp came in. After hearing her sing, Sharp went up to introduce herself and she asked Faith for a demonstration tape. Faith sent it in and to her utter delight Warner Brothers soon offered her a record contract. To this day, she has remained with the company.

From the very beginning, she helped plan her own career. Other singers let their managers or representatives make many decisions

One night in 1992, Faith was singing at the Bluebird Cafe when Martha Sharp from Warner Bros. came in.

It took longer than Faith had imagined to make a career in the music business.

for them. But Faith Hill wants in on the action. Sharp remembers, "She had her own ideas from the very beginning about how she wanted to do it."

And Faith has said, "It's definitely my show. I'm in charge." She likes to be nice, but she's ambitious, too. And she doesn't mind speaking up for herself.

In her free time, in the early '90s, Faith tried to find her birth mother, the woman who gave her up for adoption so many years earlier. Her hunt would end in 1993 after years of research. To this day, Faith Hill protects her birth mother's privacy, refusing to tell reporters her name. She has said, however, that meeting her mother has made her very happy. They remain in touch, getting together from time to time. The Perrys will always be Faith's family, but she's glad to have a chance to learn about her roots, too.

At about the same time she met her birth mother, Faith and Dan Hill divorced. After the divorce was granted,

From the very beginning, Faith helped plan her own career at Warner Bros.

she kept using Hill as her last name because she had already begun to use it as a singer.

In 1993, she also performed for the first time at the Grand Ole Opry and released her first album, entitled *Take Me As I Am.* It included a single, "Wild One," that was number one on the charts for four weeks in early 1994, being played more on the radio than any other country song. No female country singer had debuted with such a big hit for thirty years.

Take Me As I Am sold extremely well—it would soon go double platinum, selling two million copies. Appearances on television and touring with Reba McEntire (for whom Faith had once worked, selling merchandise to fans), Brooks & Dunn, and Alan Jackson increased her exposure. The Academy of Country Music named her the Best New Female Vocalist.

In 1995, Faith Hill released a second album, *It Matters To Me.* Recording it made her feel there was "pressure to live up to something." She had wondered whether she could match her initial success. But she didn't have to worry. This album did well, too, selling three million copies. The TNN/Music City News named her the Star of Tomorrow. Demonstrating that she was becoming known to a far larger circle of people than country music fans, *People* magazine put her on its list of "50 Most Beautiful People." She was winning recognition for her beautiful looks and sense of style, as well as for her voice. Soon the time would come when Americans would see her as a role model, too.

In 1995, *People* magazine put her on its list of "50 Most Beautiful People."

Chapter 4
Marriage and Family

After the appearance of her second album, Faith Hill began what was named the Spontaneous Combustion tour with another hot young country music star, Tim McGraw. Hill and McGraw had met in passing once or twice before, but on this tour they came to know each other well.

When the tour began, Faith Hill was engaged to a music company executive. But she broke off the engagement when she realized she was extremely attracted to Tim McGraw. He felt the same about her.

Faith met another country singer named Tim McGraw.

On the tour, they played 140 concerts together. Spontaneous Combustion was one of the year's most profitable country music tours. But it netted its stars much more than money. It changed their lives in a deeper way, too.

While on the road, acting on their attraction, Faith Hill and Tim McGraw began a romance. They would find they had a lot in common besides their love of country music. Like Hill, McGraw was raised in the deep South, in his case in southern Louisiana. They both grew up in small towns out in the countryside.

They shared an interest in sports. Faith had played basketball in high school, and today she enjoys softball and water skiing. As a child, Tim loved playing outside. He learned to ride horses while he was still very small and he played baseball while he was growing up.

And like Faith, Tim McGraw had a different biological parent than the ones

On tour, they played 140 concerts together.

who raised him. When he was 11, he discovered that his mother's husband was not his actual father. She had kept secret from him—and nearly everybody else—that his father was a professional baseball player named Tug McGraw, with whom she was once involved.

Both Faith and Tim felt that their romance was magical. They kept it secret until they married in Tim's hometown—Rayville,

Faith and Tim at the 2000 Grammy Awards.

Louisiana—on October 6, 1996, at a baseball game. From that point on, her new family would be the major focus of Faith Hill's life.

But Faith has dedicated her time and resources to giving something back. The Faith Hill Family Literacy Project, which she established with Time Warner and Warner Brothers Records helps people, including many grown-ups, to read. Faith would like to see a day when every single American can read. Illiteracy has touched her own life—her adoptive father,

Faith (pregnant) and Tim at the 33rd Academy of Country Music awards.

When Faith
and Tim
travel,
their
children go
with them.

Ted Perry, never learned to read well because he had to leave school early to help support his extremely large family.

In 1997, she began work on her third album, *Faith.* But she would stop work on it when she and Tim had their first child, a daughter named Gracie Katherine. The following year, their second child, a girl named Maggie Elizabeth, was born. After becoming a mother, Faith divided her time between her children and her career. Her roles would be intertwined, as she keeps her children near her even when she is at work. They even travel with her and Tim when they perform or make other public appearances.

Chapter 5
On Top

Three years passed between the release of Faith Hill's second and third albums. When she returned to the studio after the birth of Gracie, she felt renewed, inspired, and more mature. The result was *Faith*, released in 1998. It would sell four million copies worldwide. One of its singles, "This Kiss," topped the charts for three straight weeks. "This Kiss" made Faith Hill a crossover success when it also made it onto the top of the pop charts at number five.

Her popularity grew. She received four awards from the Academy of

Faith's big hit, "This Kiss," enabled her to cross over to the pop charts.

Country Music. She also set out on her own tour, being the headliner for the first time ever. While on the tour, she not only sang but promoted her literacy project. Fans who came to her concerts donated 25,000 books to the Faith Hill Family Literacy Project, which in turn donated them to schools, libraries, and hospitals.

Faith poses with a fan at the Fan Fair in 1996.

Faith was a huge success, but Faith Hill would do still more. She took a huge risk when she recorded her fourth album, *Breathe,* which was released in 1999. Ever since *Faith* had appeared a year earlier, she had found herself in a whirlwind of activity. She began, but did not finish *Breathe* when she started her tour. By the time she got back, she had only a few weeks left before she was due to finish *Breathe.*

But rather than ask Warner Brothers for extra time, she pushed right ahead. She had already recorded a few songs. Now she let instinct take over to choose the rest. She personally likes country, pop, gospel and rhythm and blues. So she recorded songs she describes as close to her heart. Rather than trying to make either a traditional country or pop album, she let her many sides show, recording a love song with her husband, a spiritual "There Will Come a Day", and a classic rock 'n roll tune written by Bruce Springsteen.

Breathe pleased Hill. To her delight, fans loved it, too, and her risk paid off. And there were other things that helped to make 1999 a great year for her. She got major advertising contracts from Cover Girl and Pepsi. She was featured on a VH1 *Divas* show that honored Diana Ross.

In 2000, Faith Hill made entertainment news when she was called in at the last possible moment to perform at the Academy Awards.

In 1999, Faith released her next hit album, *Breathe*.

Despite having just two rehearsals, she impressed the audience when she sang "Somewhere Over the Rainbow."

That year, she and McGraw also went on a new tour, called Soul2Soul. Their concerts sold out in all 42 cities where they played and got great reviews. And most importantly, they did it all as a family. Faith and Tim took Gracie and Maggie along with them, as well as a full-time nanny. They traveled in a caravan of trucks and trailers which carried 110 crew members and musicians along with their equipment. Faith said during the tour that she could not do it without her children.

One of her backup singers said, "I've seen Faith change a diaper three minutes before she walks onstage." When their mom was onstage, singing solos or duets with their daddy, the girls would play backstage.

Soul2Soul brought in more money than any other country music tour in 2000. When it ended, Faith Hill went home with her family to their house outside of Nashville. But their life hardly slowed. In 2001, Faith Hill was on top of the world. She won the American Music Academy's awards for favorite country album, favorite country female, and favorite pop/rock female. Then she received four Grammy awards.

Tim McGraw remained a huge star, too. As a celebrity couple, they found themselves often in the news. Sometimes this annoyed them, but in general they were able to laugh off rumors that circulated about them.

Today Faith Hill is a household name. Her CDs have sold more than 15 million copies. But one day that may seem a small number. Looking to the future, she says, "Now that I'm in the midst of a successful career, I want to do even more. I want it to get even bigger."

In 2001, Faith received numerous awards, including four Grammys and several from the American Music Academy.

Discography

Take Me as I Am (1993) Warner Bros.
It Matters to Me (1995) Warner Bros.
Faith (1998) Warner Bros.
Breathe (1999) Warner Bros.

Chronology

- 1967, born on September 21 in Jackson, Mississippi.
- 1972, starts school.
- 1974, sings in public for the first time at a mother-daughter banquet.
- 1985, graduates from high school. After one semester at community college, she moves to Nashville, where she hopes to make it big in the music business.
- 1988, marries Dan Hill
- 1992, is discovered by a Warner Brothers Records executive while singing in Nashville.
- 1993, meets her biological mother for the very first time, divorces her husband, and releases her first album, *Take Me As I Am*.
- 1995, releases her second album, *It Matters to Me*.
- 1996, marries fellow country music star Tim McGraw.
- 1999, wins four Academy of Country Music Awards.
- 2000, featured on VH1's *Divas 2000: A Tribute to Diana Ross*, a television special.
- 2001, wins four awards at the Grammys. Interviewed in a Barbara Walters special.

Index